Love IS THE REAL DEAL

Living Life in God's Favor

LARRY SCHLOTFELT

ISBN: 1460935624
ISBN 13: 9781460935620

II

IN DEDICATION

This book is dedicated to those who have been faithful to the Sunday school and Bible memory classes I have had the privilege of teaching. Looking back on those special times, I recognize the LOVE exhibited in their support... especially to those who got themselves out of bed early on Friday mornings to quote scripture.

A special thank you goes to those who have read my first two books, "The Bible Makes Sense", and "All the Fullness of God" and have given me such positive feedback and encouragement.

CONTENTS

DEDICATION V

INTRODUCTION VII

CHAPTER 1 *LOVE DEFINED*.. 1

CHAPTER 2 *THE PATH TO RIGHTEOUSNESS* 7

CHAPTER 3 *BEYOND DENOMINATIONS* 11

CHAPTER 4 *LOVE & SUBMISSION* 15

CHAPTER 5 *SURPASSING KNOWLEDGE*..................................23

CHAPTER 6 *GOOD GOD IN TRYING TIMES* 27

CHAPTER 7 *LOVE OR PARISH*..39

CHAPTER 8 *IN SUMMARY* 45

INTRODUCTION

To those of you who have read one of my first books, either *"The Bible Makes Sense"* or *"All the Fullness of God"*, some of this introduction may seem repetitive. However, I think it is necessary in order to establish just who I am and how I came to the point of trying to become an author so late in life.

My real credentials are that I have tried to teach the word of God for nearly forty years by simply studying the Bible. I have been teaching an adult Sunday school class for the past 37 years in two different churches. In addition, I have been involved in weekly Bible memory classes for over 23 years. The first 3 years were at Will Rogers United Methodist Church in Tulsa, OK. The remaining 20 years I taught a 6:30 AM Bible memory class on Friday mornings at Christview Christian Church. We are still members there and they are still allowing me to teach.

Though I have had no formal Bible School or seminary training, I did graduate with a bachelor's degree in Business Administration from Kansas State University in 1963. I try to never consult commentaries or study guides until I feel like I have an understanding of the Scriptures, then I might consult other resources for confirmation or additional enlightenment.

My library includes various books and Bible translations such as; King James (KJV), Revised Standard (RSV), New American Standard (NAS), Amplified Bible (AMP), and New International Version (Scriptures quoted in this book will be NIV unless noted otherwise). Commentary sources include Mathew Henry, Charles Hodge, William Barclay, James Montgomery Boice, Wycliffe, The Interpreter's Bible, various volumes of Life Application Commentary, Crossway Classic Commentaries, NIV Application Commentary, and numerous Bible dictionaries to include Vine Expository. In addition, I have compiled a library of authors that range from St. Augustine (*Confessions*) to John Calvin (*Institutes*) to Martin Luther (*Bondage of the Will*) to John Wesley (*Growing in Grace*) to Alexander Campbell (*The Christian System*), to Kierkegaard. Of the more contemporary writers I've read, are numerous volumes by Francis Schaeffer including (*Trilogy*), John MacArthur, Billy Graham, Dietrich Bonhoeffer (*Cost of Discipleship*), Watchman Nee (*The Spiritual Man*), J.B. Phillips (*Your God is too Small*), Pope John Paul II (*Crossing the Threshold of Hope*), numerous books by R.C. Sproul & Charles Stanley, Charles Spurgeon, C.S. Lewis (*Mere Christianity*), and A.W. Tozer (*Attributes of God*), among many others. The books singled out I have read at least once in their entirety.....some two & three times.

The authors who influenced me the most were the ones who convinced me they were completely in harmony with Holy Scripture. I may not have been enlightened in exactly the same way, but I was satisfied that the Bible was the basis of their perception.

The reason for mentioning just some of the authors and their works is not meant to impress anyone, but to convey the fact that I attempted to gain insight from very credible sources. I am convinced that all of the authors mentioned exemplify Spirit filled men of God.

CHAPTER 1

LOVE DEFINED

My conversion experience occurred on a porch swing when I was eight years old. I cried out to God trying to get assurance that I would go to Heaven. I had been told by a devout Christian family that you could know such a thing. Although I considered it impossible to be so sure, I was astounded at their peace and confidence. To make a long story short, after an afternoon of seeking that same assurance, God gave it to me via a warm feeling that you would have to experience to understand. I have never forgotten that incident or feared physical death since.

Early in my study of the Protestant Reformation movement, I was introduced to the concept of being saved by grace through faith and I came to recognize that as what took place on the porch swing. Although I couldn't describe it in just those terms at the time, that is what happened. I cried out to God and by his grace He gave me a new birth.

As I started to teach the Bible, I placed major emphasis on being justified by faith, and faith alone. I acknowledged love and yet in my mind and in my speech, I found it awkward to say "I love you Lord". Every time I forced myself to say those words, it required an effort that disturbed me.

It was easy to teach on faith but hard to teach on love... something was wrong. This book is to convey what I learned over the years that changed my mind-set completely.

In the New Testament (NT) there are two Greek words that have been translated into the English word love. One is *agape*, which is the unconditional love God has for us, expressing his deep and abiding interest in our well being. The other is *phileo* which is the friendship brotherly kind of Love. Although I am not a Greek scholar, I can marry up a Vine's Greek dictionary with a Berry Interlinear Text and get the gist of which word is under consideration. Why doesn't the Greek word *eros* (from which we get the word erotica), show up in the NT? We will cover that subject in chapter 4.

AGAPE GOD & AGAPE MAN

The Old Testament (OT) has a number of commands; most people are at least aware of ten of them, but the NT also has a number of commands. We will look at some of them throughout this book. The two commands that are the most important to God are recorded in Mark 12:30-31. Here we see *agape* love having a vertical and horizontal component. First and foremost, the vertical love that we direct back to God must be the same vertical component that comes down from Him. Rom. 8:38-39 depicts God's *agape* love and says nothing can stop it...it is unconditional and ever lasting. In addition, the horizontal component that we are to exhibit toward mankind is the same *agape* type love...it should also have the same qualities.

As a Christian grows spiritually, somewhere along the line, he will be exposed to First Corinthians chapter thirteen in the Bible. It is frequently referred to as the "love" chapter. The 13th verse says that love is greater than faith. It took me a while to comprehend that but when I did, it suddenly became easy to state in my mind and in my speech, "I love you Lord". My mind-set has gown in spirit to the point that it is the natural/supernatural thing to say. Now I unashamedly say it frequently throughout the day. I wonder how many other Christians have, or have had that same difficulty?

If Satan can keep the carnal Christian wary of expressing that *agape* love back to God, he probably thinks he still has the possibility of destroying a believer's faith. I am convinced that once the vertical bond is established with *agape* love going both ways, Satan is defeated and he will flee from you. James 4:7-8 makes a statement confirming that fact.

HOW GOD GRADES OUR SINCERITY

Rom. 12:9 states that "love must be sincere". A few years ago, a survey was taken to identify the most popular book of the Bible. In this particular study, the fourteenth chapter of John's gospel was the big winner The discourse here takes place at the last supper and Christ is preparing the disciples for life after he is no longer in their physical presence. There are two passages in this chapter that give clear understanding of how God is going to judge the sincerity of our love.

Verse 15. *"If you love me, you will obey what I command"*.

Verse 23. *"If anyone loves me, he will obey my teaching"*.

The love that God honors is clearly tied to obedience. Therefore, though we are saved by grace through faith (Eph. 2:8-9), God expects more from us. We also have to give credence to the next verse (Eph. 2:10)...which claims we are "God's workmanship, created (born again) in Christ Jesus to do good works". So the question becomes, obedient to exactly what? In the Great Commission (Mt. 28:20), he refers to his commandments as being the criteria.

3

We know that he is not referring entirely to the Ten Commandments or any other OT precept because Rom. 10:4 tells us that "Christ is the end of the law". The law of Mosses has no relevance pertaining to requirements for our salvation. The Ten Commandments are valuable to us only because they reflect the character of God and give us moral guidance and restraint. More importantly, there are a lot of NT commandments given to Christians this side of the cross that have to be considered.

The very great benefit of becoming a Christian is that the Holy Spirit of God himself enters our being. It is He who gives us the guidance we need toward obedience. This gift of the Holy Spirit was made available to all mankind at Pentecost (Acts 2:38) and was the fulfillment of at least two OT prophecies, (Joel 2:28 & Ezek 36:27). This union of God's Spirit with our spirit has to happen for one to legitimately call himself a Christian. Rom. 8:9 says that if you do not have the Spirit of Christ, you do not belong to Christ. A paraphrase might be; if you do not recognize the Holy Spirit in your being, you may need to go back to square one and seek a born again experience.

With the Holy Spirit dwelling within us, displaying our love through obedience takes on a new perspective. Now obedience is not something we have to do to please God, it is something we want to do. In my life, I have taught the Bible for nearly forty years not because I had to, but because I wanted to. I didn't get up early to spend time in study and prayer because I had to, but because I wanted to. As a family, we didn't set aside ten percent of our income to worship God with our finances because we had to, but because we wanted to. Over the years, a number of people suggested I write a book. Until a couple of years ago, it was the farthest thing from my mind. Then I walked into my quiet room one morning and was immediately given the desire to write one...this is my third effort...you get the point.

It is one thing to say "Lord I love you" using only your mouth and quite another thing to demonstrate that love through obedience. God's response to our being disobedient is described in the Sermon on the Mount. (Matt. 7:21-27) Check it out! It is kind of scary to just give him lip service.

CHAPTER 2

THE PATH TO RIGHTEOUSNESS

The Sunday school class I teach is called the Promises Class and we try to make ourselves aware of the many promises in scripture. One of the most important shows up in James 1:12.

> "Blessed is the man who perseveres under trial, because when He has stood the test, he will receive the crown of life that God has promised to those who love him".

There are a number of things covered in this small passage, but the one I want to dwell on is that love is connected directly to eternal life. James makes it look like we might be justified by love rather than by faith. Faith doesn't appear in this passage, yet we are promised eternal life if we persevere in our love for God. So which is it, faith or love, or both?

I contend that it is both, because I don't think they can be separated. Our human spirit, which is capable of being united with God's Holy Spirit (1 Cor. 6:17), was created with a capacity to love. That being the case, our spirit, which is personal, could never expect saving faith in something

7

impersonal such as an idol made of wood or stone. God is personal and he has made provision for us to have a loving personal relationship with him. That provision requires us to have faith in him and on what Christ accomplished for us on the cross.

Since scripture calls us to both, we simply have to include love in the formula for justification. I am not trying to change being justified by faith, I am trying to show that both faith and love are so intertwined that you can't claim one without the other. A genuine Christian could never make the statement that he loved the Lord but didn't believe in him or that he believed in him from the heart but didn't love him. When we are outside on a sunny day, we expect both heat and light from that big round ball in the sky. You cannot separate heat and light in the sunshine. So it is with becoming a Christian, you can't have a saving relationship with God without both faith and love in the mix.

THE ONLY THING THAT COUNTS

This connection is emphatically spelled out in Gal. 5:6. Here the apostle Paul is admonishing the church at Galatia not to get caught up in matters on the periphery such as circumcision, but to concentrate on the **only thing that counts** which "is **faith** expressing itself through **love**". If that was sound advice for the early church why is it not sound advice for today? I believe that it is.

My conversion experience was initiated by a Pentecostal family, I went forward and accepted Christ publically at a Baptist revival, and I was baptized by immersion at an independent Christian church. In addition, I attended a Presbyterian church infrequently in college, but spent 12 active years in a United Methodist Church. During most of those latter years I taught the Bible in an adult Sunday school class. Looking back, I thank God for the experience of becoming acquainted with believers in each denomination. In every case, faith expressing itself through love was exhibited without reference to the sign posted on the building.

I sincerely believe that the biggest problem in all of Christendom is that to the secular world, we look like a bunch of nuts that can't get our act together. I watch Christian television a lot and if I were on the outside trying to evaluate this Christianity business, I would more than likely be turned off and disgusted with the whole thing. We have a tendency to convey the message that we don't get along with each other. Some preachers appear openly hostile to anyone not exactly in agreement with their brand of Christianity. The main reason we don't appear united is because we have taken our eyes off the cross. Jesus Christ and Him crucified, is about the only thing we can agree on, but we seem to emphasize things on the periphery.

Unfortunately, the cross has taken a back seat to such contentious things as "speaking in tongues", "once saved, always saved", "seed faith", (which comes across as getting a return on an investment), and that if we go to church we are entitled to be entertained. We wouldn't dare talk about the wrath of God or anything disapproving. It might not be socially acceptable. Anything negative might be offensive. It is no wonder the secular world is confused. I am not suggesting we shouldn't discuss these controversial topics, but I am suggesting that it be done in a classroom setting with the Bible at hand.

Over the years, I have dealt with all the issues just mentioned. In every case I taught the controversial subjects to mature Christians with the provision that we use the Bible as final authority and not rely on what some teacher says... to include me. When I approach such a topic, I draw a big cross on the board behind me and make sure that it is our ultimate focus. Whether the class agrees or disagrees with me is not too important. The important thing is that we never let periphery issues take our eyes off the cross. I always state at the beginning of the class that if the discussion gets heated, we are coming back to the cross and Jesus Christ. In nearly forty years of teaching I have never had a problem with controversial subject matter.

The core message is "the only thing that counts is faith expressing itself through love". How could it be any easier to understand?

CHAPTER 3

BEYOND DENOMINATIONS

In my study of scripture, I have found no bias in favor of one denomination over the other. In fact, there is no scriptural basis for denominations whatsoever that I can detect. However, in today's culture, we have to deal with them because they affect how the world views the church at large. Since we know we can't agree and look unified across the board, we should emphasize the areas where we can be united and de-emphasize the areas where we are in disagreement.

I guess denominations are necessary since believers tend to congregate with other believers who make them comfortable. In addition, we couldn't all get in one church building. However, the problem is accentuated by the tendency to convey the message that we are the only real Christians over here at our church. Some Protestants think Catholics are doomed, some Catholics think Protestants are doomed, and I don't know what the Orthodox think, but I am sure they have an opinion...or they would be Protestant or Catholic. How foolish we look to those outside the faith.

I find it interesting that at the beginning of the first letter to the Corinthians and at the end of the second letter to the same folks, Paul calls for unity. In 1 Cor.1:10, his plea is for them "all to agree with one another so that there be no division among you and that you be perfectly united in mind and thought". In closing the second letter, he pleads for them to "Aim for perfection...to be of one mind" (2 Cor. 13:11). Somewhere, somehow those petitions have either been ignored or dismissed as not being relevant to the modern church. As best as we can, we ought to restore them.

EXPANDING GOD'S FAVOR

When we examine love from this side of the cross we see that it has a number of Christ's character qualities attached to it. We know this because God is love, (1 John 4:16). Note; God is love, but love is not God...We're not to worship love, we are to worship God. Many in secular society and even some in church think that if they can simply love people, that will make them right with God regardless of their acceptance of Christ. That pretence will not hold up in a careful study of scripture.

The qualities of *agape* love are spelled out in 1 Cor. 13:4-7.

Love is patient, love is kind. It does not envy, it does not boast, it is not proud. It is not rude, it is not self seeking, it is not easily angered, and it keeps no record of wrongs. Love does not delight in evil but rejoices with the truth. It always protects, always trusts, always hopes, and always perseveres.

These are the traits we should exhibit each and every day if we have the Holy Spirit living within us.

For the last decade or so, Christview Christian Church has provided a real look at Christmas through a production entitled Bethlehem Walk. It is a program whereby people can move through various scenes of the virgin birth. Travelers encounter shepherds in the field, wise men, and Roman guards. In addition, they pass through a typical Palestinian village before arriving at the manger scene. There are a lot of animals involved to include a camel. It is a large task for a small church and every year we have volunteers from other church denominations participate. We can unite when we concentrate on the real message of the season. I wish the unbelieving world could see how Christians can come together when we focus on things that really matter.

Now that we have defined love and examined some of its specifics, let's look at the various ways it should show up in the believer's life.

A. **Love** is the first characteristic in the fruit of the Spirit (Gal. 5:22-23), followed by joy, peace, patience, kindness, goodness, faithfulness, gentleness, and self control. These character traits should be evident in our every day behavior. My morning prayer is to ask for a fullness of His Spirit emphasizing each individual attribute. People I come in contact with should see all of these qualities in my disposition. This is hard to do because we are all so far from being perfect, but Jesus said we would be known by the fruit we bare (Matt. 7:20).

B. In Col 3:12-14, we discover **Love** being the binding force for bringing compassion, kindness, humility, gentleness, patience, forbearance, and forgiveness into perfect unity.

C. Faith and **Love** are hooked up again along with a number of character qualities in 2 Pet. 1: 11. We are called to exemplify these traits in "increasing measure" in order to insure our "rich welcome into the eternal kingdom of our Lord and Savior Jesus Christ".

D. In 1Cor.13:13 we are informed that three major aspects of our Christian walk remain: faith, hope, and love, But the greatest of these is **Love**.

When I first thought of a title for this book, I came up with "Love is the Big Deal". Then I changed it to "Love is the Real Deal" because I thought it was catchier. A more accurate description of what I want to convey would be entitled "**<u>LOVE IS THE REAL BIG DEAL</u>**".

CHAPTER 4

LOVE AND SUBMISSION

In today's world, submission is almost a dirty word. It seems to convey the meaning that someone's rights have been stomped on and nothing is more important than "my rights". No matter what the Bible says, if there is a chance it will infringe on "my rights", it has to be bad. That prevailing attitude is responsible for removing prayer from our schools, the Ten Commandments from public display, and general disrespect for authority of any kind. It has been especially prevalent in the home where the wife has been taught that in secular society she should never exhibit a compliant attitude. If the man is submissive, it seems to be OK. I want us to look at what the Bible says about submission and how it relates especially to love in the family.

First, submission on the part of everyone is the product of wisdom from above. Godly wisdom calls us in general to be submissive (James 3:17). It is wise to submit to the police officer trying to pull you over. It is wise to submit to your boss who is giving you directions you don't want to follow (but only up to the point where it doesn't violate scripture). And yes, it is wise for the husband to be submissive to the wife's advice even though Eph. 5:22 calls on the wife to "submit to your husband as to the Lord". There have been plenty of times when it was wise for me to submit to Carol's suggestions. On many occasions, her insight was the right one and most of the time I have been sensible enough to see it. The man who is astute is the one who always has the consent and agreement of his spouse before making major decisions. You have probably heard the counsel from an unknown source..."if mama ain't happy, ain't nobody happy". It is the wise man who understands and adheres to this sage advice.

This particular passage (Eph. 5:22), must cause the women's liberation movement to go right through the ceiling, but let's look a little deeper into the message. Before Paul singles out the wife, he spoke of being generally "submissive to one another out of reverence for Christ" in v.21. This fits in with the wisdom part of submission coming from James, but here Paul does go deeper into the position of the wife in the family environment.

I am sorry if this offends, but the word declares that the husband is to be the head of the family unit. Don't be angry with me if you don't like what the Bible says, I didn't write it. Take it up with God. Going back to the basics of "all scripture is inspired by God" (2 Tim 3:16 KJV), and he "cannot lie" (Titus 1:2 KJV), this arrangement is God ordained whether we like it or not. If we do not properly adhere to it, we are violating a holy precept.

However, if you read farther in scripture to Eph 5:25, you will see that the requirements for the husband are even more strict. We are to love our wives as Christ loved the church and gave himself for it. That is agape love in both cases. From what I have observed in my lifetime, God's formula works whether or not it is politically correct. As Christians, political correctness should never trump God's word. His word should always be our guide. The successful marriages I have observed all fit this mold. If both the husband and the wife get their relative positions in order and are obedient to their respective tasks, I don't see a problem.

The main player is this scenario is the husband. If he indeed loves the wife as Christ loves the church, and seeks and follows wisdom from above, I don't think the wife will have a problem with his leadership. The problems come when the husband tries to lead or dominate things without the Godly wisdom to consult his wife and take her position into consideration. So, the bigger burden is on the husband. The wife can and should support every family situation with prayer.

Major decisions made within a marriage require harmony between the partners. For instance, the decision to buy a new house should not be the result of one partner demanding the other to submit to his or her choice. Such a physical structure has little chance of becoming a happy home. In our marriage, Carol and I have determined the big decisions need to be made after a lot of prayer. Ask God for guidance then wait for some assurance of your being led. Look for "open doors" and "closed doors".

The best examples I can relate are associated with home buying. In the early 1980s we made a decision to build a new house. We made a verbal agreement with a contractor and had everything in place for a formal closing scheduled for a Saturday morning. He never showed up and we have not heard from him to this day. We certainly got the closed door message and adhered to the will of God. A few years later, we tried it again, but this time we prayed a little differently. This time we "put out a fleece". Our approach in prayer was to propose a sales price on our existing home that we thought was fair, set a minimum taking price, limit the process to six months and see what happened. If it sold within those parameters, we would take that as an "open door" and proceed. The first person who looked at the house bought it at the asking price and paid cash without a quibble. We were confident that was an answer to our prayer and we moved on to buy the house we live in today.

Looking back on those two episodes, putting God in position to guide us removed any need for one of us to be in submission to the other. We put God on the throne and asked him to show us the way. He did and we have never been sorry about the outcome. He gave us the wisdom and provision we needed to buy a perfect house for us, all things considered.

SUBMISSION & EROS LOVE

As I mentioned earlier, the Greek word *eros*, from which we derive the word erotica, does not show up in the NT. I used to wonder why God did not give us specifics of what could and could not be done in the bedroom. I have come to a peace about that question by examining the freedom we receive from the Holy Spirit living within us. 2 Cor. 3:17 says that "where the Spirit of the Lord is, there is freedom". We know that erotic love is necessary for us to marry and procreate. Marriage is of God and one of the ways we know which man or woman to marry is whether or not that *eros* love is present. The secular world calls it "chemistry" or "a connection", or "magic". Something in both the man and woman has to spark in order for that eros love to take effect. We are designed by God with a sexual appetite; it simply has to be controlled. None of this violates scripture as long as the sexual part is done in the bedroom of husband and wife. The Bible says the wedding bed is not to be defiled (Heb. 13:4 KJV) in the NIV it says "kept pure". Note: there is more to picking a marriage partner than just the physical and/or "chemistry" factor, but it needs to be there.

BEWARE; I have described a situation in which Satan will try to deceive the Christian. Sexual immorality is one of his strongest weapons. Just as he deceived Eve into thinking God's words could be circumvented, he will try to convince the world that sex outside marriage is not only to be expected but in today's world can't be resisted. Believe me it can be resisted...Carol and I can testify to the fact.

There can be no doubt about it; God is adamantly opposed to sex outside of marriage...PERIOD. No politically correct blather in rebuttal please. He is so against it that in the OT times, it was punishable by death (Lev. 20:10). Somewhere along the line, society decided that was too harsh a punishment and now we have come to the place where it is not condemned but is embraced and encouraged. Just turn on your TV and watch any prime time program that the industry said they would monitor and keep pure in the early evening hours. A former President of the United States who was involved in a colossal sexual scandal is currently reported to receive $100,000 for certain private appearances. Just a few days ago, ESPN released the results of a poll taken to identify America's favorite athlete. It was a golf pro who is still in the middle of trying to resolve family problems resulting from a number of his adulterous affairs. We have come a long way to the place where socially accepted decadence is the norm rather than the exception.

Sexual perversion being what it is today, how does *eros* fit into the married life of the believer? I acknowledge submission to be a common requirement for both husband and wife. Further, I consider freedom to be a gift of the Holy Spirit. The conclusion I come to is that anything the husband and wife agree to is OK as long as it is kept within the confines of marriage. In addition, one partner should never try to force anything that the other finds offensive. That would violate the call to be submissive to one another. As long as it fits into God's parameters, *eros* love is to be enjoyed by husband and wife. This is as God intended, and it works.

It is critical to the point that it needs to extend well into married life. As far back as I can remember, we have tried to have a "date night" every week giving it high priority on our "things to do" list. With the prevalence of discount movies, it does not have to get too expensive. In addition, ever since we were able to make it happen, we have taken little "you and me" mini-vacations (no kids). It may have been only an overnight at a local hotel to a week in Bermuda, but every year we made sure we got away to spend a few days by ourselves. I believe those two things are vital to a successful marriage and should be pursued with diligence.

This is not to suggest that the mini-vacations replace family ones. Family vacations have always been a high priority. We all made it to Europe twice; Hawaii once and even took our children and their spouses on a couple of Caribbean cruises. We also visited Disney World and Branson a few times in the mix.

If God's game plan is adhered to; just think of how the divorce rate would go down, spouses would not have to compare their bedroom performances with anyone else, abortions would decrease, sexually transmitted diseases would disappear, and maybe we could start trusting our politicians again.

As I look back on our married life and the way it has been described, it might appear that it has all been easy going until our health issues came into being. The answer is that blessings have overcome adversities all along the way. I now see the providential hand of God involved in everything that has been meaningful in our marriage.

Going back to the beginning of our relationship; I first noticed Carol one day as I followed her and a high school classmate of mine walking back from our college campus to her sorority which just happened to be next to my fraternity. It was an act of God that I even lived there. Kansas State did not have men's dormitories in those days. If they had, I probably would never have joined a fraternity in the first place. I didn't know it at the time, but my friend and Carol were roommates and she arranged our first date. This was in February of 1961 and we were married that September. I don't suggest that everyone get married after such a short courtship, but in our situation, it worked out better than I could have ever imagined.

One of the reasons we sensed a degree of urgency was because Carol was to graduate in May and needed some direction for her immediate future. I was behind her in school because I changed my college major from Architecture to Business Administration (those drawing classes didn't transfer very well and I fell a little behind).

After we got married, we had a short honeymoon and headed back to college to search for jobs and a place to live. Our first apartment consisted of the entire attic of a small residence. The only partition in the entire area was one to separate the bathroom from the living part. It was so small that the bed had to be positioned under the gabled roof in such a way that you were required to crawl into a sleeping position. You couldn't sit up in bed at all.

Carol found a job at the Singer Sewing Center in downtown Manhattan, KS and I got a part time job at Sears, also downtown; so after a few months we found another apartment where we could both walk to work. (She didn't like to drive having gotten a less than adequate Drivers Ed class in high school. Her instructor broke his leg at the point where he should have given her hands on experience in the car...she passed her class with an A grade and never got behind the wheel). That next apartment was two small rooms in a basement, but you could set up in bed...the only problem was that the bed was also the couch. Most of our entertainment was playing games with friends. It was the latter part of this experience when we got our first TV...small and black & white.

After year and a half of this existence, I graduated and received a commission as a 2nd Lt. in the US Army. We were off to Ft. Benning, GA where I attended the Infantry Officers Basic Course and awaited orders to flight school. We made the trip in a 1954 Chevrolet that required us to fill it up with oil nearly as often as with gas. After finishing the infantry course, I was given the meaningless job as a tactical officer for some recruits. The unofficial job description was to get them rounded up in the morning, send them off for training, then play pool and ping pong until they arrived back in the late afternoon. I got pretty good at both sports. However, I did get one troubling letter while in the midst of this waiting period. I was initially assigned to the 82nd Airborne Division in Ft. Bragg, NC. This was to occur after I graduated from flight school. The letter was from an enterprising colonel from the 82nd suggesting I go to jump school since I was right there at Ft. Benning sort of in limbo. I wrote him a nice letter back and told him I intended to fly airplanes and not jump out of them and if I was still assigned to them after flight school, I might consider it...after I had my wings. By the grace of God I never had to pursue the matter any further.

There is more personal testimony in my other two books, but I want to summarize how I see LOVE as it pertains to a God ordained marriage. First of all, as you know the New Testament was written in Greek. I know of at least four Greek words that have been translated into our English word LOVE. They are:

1. Agape...describes the unconditional love God has for us.

2. Phileo...covers brotherly love that occurs between friends

3. Storge...illustrates the love in a family

4. Eros...deals with our erotic nature

Of the four, only Agape and Phileo are mentioned specifically but the other two are certainly implied. When we as Christians say the word "love" to our spouse, as in, "I love you", I am convinced there have to be elements of all four incorporated. The word of God supports that contention.

CHAPTER 5

SURPASSING KNOWLEDGE

In 1 Cor. 13:8-12 the Apostle Paul makes reference to a time when prophecies, tongues, and knowledge will pass away. I have heard that passage used to discredit the gift of tongues. The idea being that after the Bible was written, prophecy, knowledge, and tongues ceased. I don't think that makes sense when we consider the high esteem Paul places on knowledge in some of his other letters. (I do believe the gift of tongues is valid for this lifetime even though it is not a gift I possess. I discuss the matter of tongues in depth in my book, "All the Fullness of God"). It seems to me this passage is in dealing with the eternal destiny of a Christian. When "perfection comes" (v.10) i.e. we pass from this life, we will "know fully" (v.12) all we need to know. In the meantime, let's take a little deeper look at love as it pertains to knowledge.

PAUL'S 2 PRAYERS

His prayer for the church at Philippi (Phil. 1:9-11) is that their "love might abound more and more in knowledge and depth of insight". This links love to knowledge big time. It stands to reason, if you think about your individual walk with Christ. The more knowledge you have about God, the more likely you will be led to a place of "knowing God".

23

There is a difference between head knowledge and heart knowledge. A lot of people know about him, but only a Christian has the privilege of knowing him. (John 17:3 links knowing him to eternal life; it doesn't mention knowing about him). The more we know him, the greater the love we have for him. As I mentioned in chapter one, it took awhile for me to get comfortable about expressing my love back to God. The more I got to know him, the easier it became to convey those feelings in his presence.

Anyone who has expressed love to another human being has probably faced a similar situation. It likely took some time before the words "I love you" could be exchanged comfortably. As the relationship becomes more intimate, the words come easier. I think it is the same with God; the more time we spend with him, the closer the relationship, the greater the love we share and the more open we are about it. (This same principle applies as we convey love to members of our family)

I am a big believer in quiet times. Over the years, I have developed the habit of getting up early in the morning and spending quality time with the Lord. During my working years, our normal routine was to get up at 4:15 AM during the week in order to have at least an hour for study and prayer. Now in retirement, the only thing that has changed is I can get up earlier and I don't have to stop and go to the office. (This is my third book since I retired and they have all been written between 2 AM and 8 AM) If you are reading this and cannot identify a knowing relationship with God, it will be because you have not spent enough quiet time in his presence. Ps. 46:10 calls us to "be still and know that I am God'.

Paul's prayer in his letter to the Ephesians links faith and love together again and attaches them to knowledge of the fullness of God (Eph. 3:16-19). In "*All the Fullness of God*", I used this passage as the foundation for its content.

Not only does he speak of love, he speaks of a love that surpasses knowledge. It implies that the love of Christ is so big that we cannot come to grips with it. It is described as being too "wide and long and high and deep" for us to get our arms around. He then prays that the Ephesians might know that love in order to reach spiritual fulfillment. Just as the Bible provides for us a "peace that passes understanding" (Phil 4:7 KJV), now we are to look for a "love that surpasses knowledge" (Eph.3:19). These things are hard to explain, they have to be experienced. I am no super Christian, but I can testify to both being true. It just takes being in his presence over time.

This love is further described in Rom. 8:38 as a love that nothing can deter or interfere with. Paul was convinced that: "neither death nor life, neither angels nor demons, neither the present nor the future, nor any powers, neither height nor depth, nor anything else in all creation will be able to separate us from the love of God that is Christ Jesus our Lord".

God has his love firmly in place. We need to strive for that same kind of love. That is how we come to understand the deep things of God. They are revealed to us by his Spirit. We are set apart for this blessing because of our love for him (1 Cor. 2:9-10). This is how we grow spiritually; this is how we arrive at the fullness of God.

Love really is a big deal.

CHAPTER 6

GOOD GOD IN TRYING TIMES

As I start this chapter, Carol and I find ourselves in a transition stage of life. We have just made the decision to move to a retirement community. Our thought has always been that we would stay in our home until we felt the call to move. We sought guidance from above on timing after having cleaned out both our parent's houses when they became disabled. That was not a burden we wanted to pass on to our children.

As of a few days ago we both became convinced that God was moving us in a definite direction. We see God's answer to prayer and I will share some of the details. One might call it a "*Holy Irony*" that we are undergoing this experience at the same time this chapter came up for consideration.

****

There is a break here of approximately five months in the composition of this manuscript. The move is over and we are very happy in our new surroundings. More important, we are still confident that we are here as a result of our obedience to divine guidance. That assurance brings about a peace in the matter even though we had to deal with some very trying times in the process.

****

Since day one of our marriage, I have been convinced that we enjoy the best union possible in this lifetime. I haven't seen one I would trade for in the nearly fifty years we have been together (we will enter our 50th year in 2011). Having said that, I will also tell you our marriage has never been tested like it was in this recent move. One might ask, "if the move was orchestrated by God, why the turmoil"? Stay with me, and I will answer that question as the story unfolds.

As has been mentioned, we never make a big move without feeling the presence of God. We pray for open doors and closed doors along with some sign that we are making an acceptable decision. I will try to put this whole venture in perspective with those criteria in mind. Luck and coincidence cannot be considered when we acknowledge the providence of God.

For the past few years, it has weighed on my mind that we should at least consider moving to an environment where health issues could be addressed as we grow older and weaker in this mortal body. In the spring of this year, I made those concerns known to Carol, but she wasn't interested. She wanted to stay in our home and for what appeared to be good reason. Our house is paid for and our retirement income was such that we were comfortable financially. We were able to travel as much as we wanted to and my health issues were pretty much under control. Why then should we put ourselves in a position where we would have to pay dollars out every month for a new place to live? On the surface, it didn't make much sense. I had been praying about the situation but hadn't made a big deal about it. The Lord impressed on me that when the time was right, we would both be in agreement.

Within a couple of months of this early discussion, we started getting invitations from two very nice retirement communities to come have lunch and tour their facilities. We sort of let the first offers pass, but the idea was planted.

Carol was agreeable that at least we should see what was available and get a free meal. Without me pressing the issue, she was at least showing some curiosity. Because we had to place her mother in a nursing home a number of years ago, we had already visited a lot of the facilities around Tulsa. (Her mother is still with us at 105 years young)

Our first semi-serious interest was in the cottages associated with the community where we now live. In my mind I was convinced we could acquire one of them and live happily ever after whenever the time came. A few weeks passed and we kept getting invitations. Both of us liked the lady who showed us around there so we went back and looked at the cottages again. I was having a problem figuring out how we could fit our furniture in any of the available floor plans and there just wasn't enough space for me to store books. Over the years I have built up a rather large library and the cottages did not provide a solution for that problem. While we were there for our second visit, our hostess suggested that maybe we consider a unit that was available in the large apartment complex. We were reluctant because it was a little larger, going to cost more money, and we didn't think we wanted to live in what appeared to be a hotel. However we decided to look at it.

Here is where we first realized the hand of God was giving us specific direction. As we walked into the apartment, we were both overwhelmed by the view outside a very spacious balcony. Even though this community is only two miles from a large shopping complex, we only see parts of the village and the surrounding countryside. How unique to be in the city limits, but have the feeling of living in the country. (We now speak of "going into town" when we leave the premises)

The second thing that caught our attention was that the previous owner had renovated one large wall in the dining area. It was all built-in cabinetry, much of which could be used to store books. We were concerned about the existing dark stain, but were assured we could select a new color to meet our satisfaction.

The third thing we discovered was the floor plan in the apartment looked like it was designed for our furniture. It appeared that our living room setting would fit in nicely which it did.

In addition, over the years, we have accumulated quite a few pieces of original and limited edition artwork. We were concerned about having enough room to display the ones we wanted to bring. Space also seemed available in this apartment for that need and we could have track lighting installed in every room to enhance the beauty of the paintings.

Now we were seeing more indication of God's direction. Things were starting to come together. Carol's attitude changed completely, book storage was not going to be a problem, the floor plan was compatible, and we were genuinely excited about apartment living after seeing the view from our third story balcony. In all these things we were in agreement. This facility just "felt right" to both of us. Even though it was to be quite different from living in our house, there was something that just made us comfortable. Everyone we talked to was friendly and encouraged us with good testimonies, both staff and residents. I have to this day not heard a negative word spoken by anyone concerning this establishment.

If we were going to be obedient to divine leading, we had to press on to analyzing the financial situation for further assurance. I will not bore you with those facts other than to tell you that we were able to make things work out to our satisfaction. I am convinced that the money going forward will not be a problem either.

God does In fact move in mysterious ways sometimes. Let me give you an aside. One Sunday shortly after we made the commitment, we walked into church on Sunday morning and were handed the church bulletin with the word "MOVE" in big capital letters on the front cover. Carol and I looked at each other in amazement. We understood the message was given to us as confirmation. The secular world calls that coincidence. We consider it to be providence. As for the church and the specific intent of the preacher, the word was meant to convey an entirely different meaning.

TRUST AND TEST

In most respects, the whole project had been enjoyable up through the commitment phase. It had been fun picking out new carpet, new paint, granite for the counter tops, and new wood stain for the cabinets. Along with the normal excitement of moving, things were going along pretty smooth. That was about to change. The actual move was to be very challenging, but God was always there to get us through. In looking back on the venture, he sustained us through many hiccups and stumbles along the way. His promise is to never leave us or forsake us (Heb. 13:5) and he never did.

Let me give you a couple of examples of how he prepared us. For the last few years we have hosted a small group one night a month in our home. We do different things but frequently use a Christian video as a basis for our discussion. One night in the beginning of this move process, one lady was to provide a video of Andy Stanley's. When it came time to put the unit in the DVD, we noticed that it was a CD and not a video disc. We ended up listening to a very inspirational talk based upon Luke 5:4-7. Since we couldn't view the program, I was much more intent in listening to it. I got the message loud and clear. God said to me that night over and over, "Trust Me". I was going to have to rely on that command big time in the next few weeks.

Another help came in the middle of the night when I was watching a Joyce Meyer program. Her subject matter was "you are going to be tested". She was quoting from 1 Cor. 10:13 which is a passage I had memorized many years ago and have hung onto before in difficult times. I needed to have it refreshed in my mind because the testing was coming.

I knew this particular move was going to be difficult because we had lived in our house for so long and had never thrown anything away. We had a complete attic floor over a two car garage and it was filled to overflowing with "stuff". In addition all four bedroom closets along with two hall closets were filled with "stuff". We were going to have to down size to a two bedroom apartment with very little storage in comparison.

There were a lot of sentimental areas that had to be dealt with. Carol's wedding dress, my military uniforms, career awards, kid's toys, sports equipment, etc. etc. All the things associated with a growing family over 26 years in the same house. We simply could not take all those things with us.

The first test involved photographs. We have taken photographs for over 49 years. Much of that time we had children and grandchildren, and then our children had spouses. In time they all took family photographs and shared their copies with us. Every major function had a large number of photos covering the event. Add to that the number of vacations Carol and I took on our own along with archive family photos going back into the eighteen hundreds and you have a lot of pictures to cull. We started that process only to recognize it was a futile effort. Too many times I wanted to throw away something that she thought was just "too cute". And conversely, some things I thought were important for my side of the family, she had little interest in because she didn't know people involved. It was the same for her side of the family. She needed to keep meaningful photos of people I didn't know. You get the picture. This was one area in which we were finally overwhelmed to the point that we just boxed up what we couldn't decide on. Those boxes are currently under the bed. That was the first test.

Overriding everything, was trying to adhere to a plan that would coordinate our actual move with the completion of the apartment renovation. That time frame was a little over 6 weeks. Remember, we're both over seventy and not moving too well and not thinking too well sometimes. We both have the problem of walking into a room on occasion and wondering why we are there.

This added pressure was getting to both of us. The task seemed at times to be beyond our ability to cope and by the end of the day, we were exhausted. It seemed like every day that we planned to accomplish a certain project; something would come along to interfere and get us behind schedule. We were always trying to catch up. However, the Lord gave me one passage of scripture that I shared with Carol about every day to keep us going. In Deut. 30:11 comes the message, "Now what I am commanding you today is not too difficult for you or beyond your reach". We were both stretched beyond what we thought were our limits. On more than one occasion tears were shed by both of us as the mountain seemed too high to climb.

However, Carol had an additional way of keeping us motivated through the scriptures. At the beginning of each day, she would bring me a number of passages she had identified the night before that were pertinent to where we were in the moving process. It may have been something we had to tackle that particular day—or something that just spoke to the situation in general. Sometimes she had a handful for us to consider. Her scriptures always got the day started properly, but I frequently had to call on the words in Deut.30:11 to make it through.

Although the challenge seemed great, we made it and I witnessed my sweet wife going way beyond what she thought she could accomplish. She has some health issues too, but on occasion, her endurance was greater than mine. Frequently she was determined to keep going when I was pooped and wanting to stop.

SOME "JUST ENOUGHS"

Some time ago in my walk with the Lord, he impressed on me that he was a God of "just enough's". Think about it. In his creation, there is "just enough" gravity so that we can get around as we do. A greater gravitational pull would require bigger muscles in order to even walk. If the pull were lessened, we might go bouncing through the air with every step. In addition, the atmospheric pressure is "just enough". If it was not, we would have trouble breathing as we do today. The distance between the earth and the sun is "just enough". If it was lessened, we would burn up and anything greater would cause us to freeze. You get the idea.

I saw some "just enough's" in this moving experience that helped confirm the fact that we were in God's will. Book storage was going to be a problem. There was an area in the guest bedroom that one of our bookcases might fit, but the space was going to be close. Guess what, there was "just enough" room. We had an expensive chandelier that we wanted to bring with us. After it got here, we discovered that the ceiling above where we wanted to place it had to be reinforced. That was going to be an expensive problem to fix unless we could move the positioning a short distance and attach the support to an existing structure. Result; there was "just enough" room to move it and still have it centered above the table. I mentioned that our living room furniture would fit into our new apartment. It does, but it is a cozy fit. There is "just enough" room so that it is esthetically pleasing and we can still move our bodies around.

God is a good God and he cares about our little problems. In 1 Pet. 5:7 He says to "Cast all your care on him because he cares for you" (KJV). All means all. Some people think God is too busy solving big problems and we shouldn't bother him with our petty desires. If you think that, your god is too small. The *agape* love we discussed earlier is "more than enough" to help us with the most meager problem we have. If we don't call on him in those instances, we are in fact being disobedient to scripture. There is a Christian song that states in the lyrics that "if I didn't have a problem, I wouldn't know my God could solve them". I think the song writer was right. It is important to know that no matter the size of the need, it is OK to cry out to God. I don't think you have to consult him on what color of socks to wear, but anything that causes anxiety should be brought to his attention.

SCAR IN THE KITCHEN

By now I hope you understand that I firmly believe in God's providence. I am convinced that nothing happens in life that God doesn't either cause to happen or allow to happen. Satan gets by with many things, but only because God gives his consent. His consent is for a purpose that Christians may or may not understand, but we should never forget the lesson of Rom.8:28... it will eventually be for our good.

Let me give you one last example of how God showed me his absolute providence in this move. As has been mentioned, we were allowed to select new granite counter tops for the kitchen. From the sample, we picked one that would harmonize with the new carpet and paint. When we viewed the finished product, we were upset that right by the sink was an area of about two square feet that was very discolored and stood out like a sore thumb. It was ugly. We didn't make an issue of it because it would take a long time to replace it and everything else in the apartment was fine. One night, in the middle the night, where I get some of my best insight, God impressed on me that the stain looked a lot like spilt blood...and it does. I now consider that scar to exemplify the scar that was placed on humankind when it took the life of Christ. Now when I see it, I think of the blood that was shed for me. Immediately, the scar in the kitchen became something that ministers to me...it is no longer ugly, it calls my attention to the love that is the subject matter of his book.

Sometimes there is a lighter side to his providence. Yesterday didn't start out too good. Carol was unhappy with me early on and all the marital friction lately has been a result of the move. In her mind, most if not all of the things that had gone wrong, were my fault; either I didn't give her enough time to sort things out, I put her under too much pressure to meet the move schedule (I may have misled her as to how difficult the schedule would be to change once it was set in motion), or I let things get away from us by not being vigilant enough in watching the movers. Some of her contentions are at least partially true because we have lost or misplaced quite a few things. Yesterday, there was an additional conflict to deal with. As we were driving her car to town in forty degree weather, the heater did not seem to be working. Bear in mind that I don't drive her car very often but I was convinced the heater operated exactly like my SUV since both vehicles were made by the same manufacturer. As I was moaning and complaining and moving all the knobs around trying to get it to come on, Carol was trying to tell me I was doing it wrong...imagine that. She even suggested I consult the owner's manual, but I refused. I was confident I knew the system and the system wasn't working. Carol was insulting my intelligence and after awhile I told her so. With that she made some remarks about my being stubborn and asked me to "please let her move this one dial to the right"...toward warmer. While I was preoccupied with driving, she sneaked a movement on the knob and guess what, after driving around all day with only the "buns warmers" for comfort, the heater miraculously started to work. I still don't understand it and may have to give in and read the manual. However, the most important thing occurred after we returned to the apartment and were recounting the day's events. There was a point where we both simultaneously erupted into what was nearly uncontrollable laughter at the absurdity of the whole day. God knew we both needed to lighten up and have a good belly laugh. He is a providential God who gave us a remedy to a small care.

CHAPTER 7

LOVE OR PARISH

There is a part of Christendom that seems to devalue or even disavow the need to be born again. There have been numerous surveys to substantiate this fact. A high percentage of respondents will claim to be Christian, but when the question is modified to "are you born again", the affirmative response is much lower. Therefore, I am satisfied that there are a lot of people claiming to be Christians who do not know the meaning of the word.

As we have already discovered, Christ's own words emphatically refute such a position (John 3:3-7). He said, "You must be born again". Just raising your hand one Sunday morning and moving to the front of the church will not save you. Neither will the simple act of baptism, without repentance (Acts 2:38). True Christianity is a spiritual matter. Jesus is not likely to visit anyone in a physical sense this side of heaven to coax you along.

The Bible teaches that we are justified by faith in Christ and by faith alone. We accept his atoning sacrifice as payment for our sin debt, confess him with our mouth, and are justified (or made right with God) in the process (Rom. 10:9-10). That confession has to come from our recognizing ourselves sinners in the eyes of a Holy, Holy, Holy God. It cannot simply be because we were brought up in the church or want to satisfy a certain individual's encouragement. We must have a deep seated desire to repent, or turn away from that sinful way of life and turn to the loving relationship one can have with God(Acts 2:38). At the time we make such a decision, we may not understand it fully, but we know something changed on the inside. The change occurs because at that time, the Holy Spirit comes into our lives to have communion with our spirit...one on one (1 Cor.6:17). If you do not recognize that communion, then you should question your status in respect to being "born again".

If you do not recognize the Holy Spirit in your inner being, you should test your faith (2 Cor.13:5). In other words, if you do not recognize the presence of the Holy Spirit, you may not be a Christian at all. He has to be there for you to legitimately call yourself a believer (Rom.8:9). His presence is a "must", as in "You must be born again" (John 3:7).

SAVED FROM WHAT

In the Christian vernacular, what I have just described is sometimes referred to as "being saved". That begs the question, "Being saved from what"?

This is a point of contention between what the Bible teaches about God, and what most of the world wants to acknowledge. The word of God clearly teaches that we are saved from the wrath of God. We all want to feel comfortable in the presence of a loving God and we do not want to think about him ever getting angry... no matter how we displease him. However, in our sinful nature we were considered to be objects of God's wrath (Eph.2:3). if we are going to get a clear picture of God's character, we must consider his wrathful side.

If one wants to get a true feeling about how God's anger is addressed toward such things as atheism and sexual perversion, you simply have to read 14 verses of Holy Scripture (Rom 1:18-32). As I write this, there is a movement trying to organize atheists in this country. They seek proper recognition so they can combat Christianity and make politicians aware of their considerable clout. The success of the gay community is their model for promoting their agenda. National exposure on ABC television is aiding their cause, so they may become a force to be reckoned with.

Consider the overall culture we live in. It glamorizes immorality and ridicules anyone who dares to be in opposition. The entertainment industry can hardly put out a program today that does not include homosexuality or sexual perversion in some form and portrays it to be the norm rather than the exception. Sex outside of marriage has become the accepted way to live. A recent survey revealed that over 40% of those interviewed considered marriage to be irrelevant.

I think the secular world believes that God, if there is a God, so loves us that no matter how much we ignore him or his teaching, he will never hold us accountable or bring about any harsh judgment...certainly no severe punishment. Much of the world does not regard an eternal Hell to be a serious consideration. Whoever comes to that conclusion simply does not know the God of the Bible. His ways are not the ways of the world (Is. 55:8-9). Where the world says perversion is alright, the Bible warns that it is wrong and if it is not brought under control will result in eternal damnation (Gal.5:19-21).

Remember, these are not my words but the words of God (2 Tim. 3:16). Every living human being today has to come to grips with this particular passage of scripture. Whether you believe it or not, it will set the stage for how you live out life on this planet. Either the Bible is the word of the living God or it is not. Yes or no. Everyone has to decide for themselves.

THE SLIPPERY SLOPE

One of America's greatest Christian thinkers was Jonathan Edwards (1707-1768) and he produced one of Christendom's most classic sermons. It is entitled "Sinners in the hands of an angry God". I know it is required reading in some seminaries but it should be required reading for every human being. There can be no doubt about it, this is a "hell-fire and brimstone" message but it is one that ought to be contemplated by everyone. It was true in the eighteenth century and it is true today.

Deut. 32:35 is the primary passage used as a basis for the message. That portion of scripture depicts man living on a slippery slope with eternal disaster close by. In Ps. 37:30 we're told that a righteous man's foot will not slip, and in Rom.4:23-24 we see true righteousness coming from our faith in God. To paraphrase; unless we repent, turn from the sinful nature we were born with, and put our faith in Christ, we remain on a slippery slope with no hope.

Jesus Christ is the only way to God the Father (John 14:6) and the wrath of a Holy God can be summed up in another verse in the Gospel of John.

John 3:36 *"Whoever believes in the Son has eternal life, but whoever rejects the Son will not see life, for God's wrath remains on him"*.

Can there be a more black and white verse in the entire Bible? Either you accept Christ or you don't. You either choose eternal life or eternal damnation. God has given everyone exposed to his word a choice and the choice is clear...and everyone who hears this message is without excuse (John 15:22). God's coming wrath is a promise (Col.3:6).

JUDGEMENT FOR ALL

Just as no one wants to consider God's wrath, the same can be said for his Judgment. However, the Apostle Paul makes it clear in 2 Cor. 5:10 that we all must make an appearance before the Judgment seat of Christ. All means all...Paul includes himself. Christians and non Christians alike will stand before God and be accountable, but there is one very big difference in the outcome. The believer's judgment has already taken place as it pertains to his eternal destiny (Col. 3:1-4). In God's eyes there is no more condemnation directed toward him and he has already crossed over from death to life...past tense... already accomplished (John 5:24). "Blessed is the man whose sin the Lord will never count against him" (Rom. 4:8). The Christian stands to be rewarded...and that is a good thing (1 Cor.3:11-13). In Christ's Sermon on the Mount, he referred to "treasures in heaven" (Mt.6:19). They are being kept in storage.

For the unbeliever or non Christian, the Judgment seat of Christ is outlined in a different context. Rewards are not mentioned, but one's eternal destiny is at stake. This is often referred to as the Great White Throne Judgment (Rev.20:11-15). If your name doesn't appear in the book of life, the result certainly depicts the wrath of an angry God. Atheists take note...the Bible just might be what it claims to be, the word of God. It would seem to be wise to consider eternal destinies now when the final outcome can still be altered.

CHAPTER 8

IN SUMMARY

Make no doubt about it, God is a loving God. In the last Chapter I emphasized a passage in Ephesians where we were referred to as objects of wrath in our sinful state (Eph. 2:3). Let me call your attention also to the next verse:

Eph. 2:4. "Because of his great LOVE for us, God who is rich in mercy made us alive with Christ even when we were dead in transgressions—it is by grace you have been saved".

This passage shows God as being rich in mercy. Refer back to Eph.1:7 and we see Him described as being rich in grace. Being rich in mercy and grace means he has a lot in store...a lot to pass around.

If we look just a little further forward in scripture, we come again to Eph. 2:8-10.

"For it is by grace you have been saved through faith—and this is not from yourselves it is the gift of God—not by works so that no man can boast. For we are God's workmanship, created in Christ Jesus to do good works which God prepared in advance for us to do".

The gospel message is pretty well covered in that passage. Salvation is being saved from wrath. Grace (God's loving kindness freely given) is God's part...faith is our part. Out of the riches of his grace and mercy he has offered the gift of eternal life to anyone who wants it. However, for the giving transaction to be complete, the gift has to be received. It is received by faith, and faith alone according to protestant doctrine.

When that reception occurs, one is described as being born again...born of the Spirit (John 3:5-7). It results in us becoming one with Christ through the uniting of His Spirit with ours (1 Cor, 6:17). This is commonly referred to by the Apostle Paul as being "in Christ" or "Christ in us". We are in fact born anew and all things become new (2 Cor. 5:17).

In my college days I was taught that one of the most important words in all of advertising was the word "new". If one could introduce a new product, a new formula, or even a new addition, you had something to get the buyers attention. I wonder why that concept is lost when it comes to announcing a "new birth" in Christ. Satan and his influence in the secular world have made it hard to get that positive message across. However it is the most important message Christians can deliver; it has eternal value.

The question to all mankind is, "Do you want eternal life in the presence of a Holy and righteous God or do you want to reject the gift in order to live a life that ignores Christ's sacrifice"? A life without Christ is a life that offers no hope for eternal bliss and will end in eternal damnation.

Today you are one day closer to that judgment seat than you were yesterday. The Bible says we have an appointment..."Once to die but after this the judgment" (Heb.9:27 KJV). The first part we have no control over; physically we may not see tomorrow. The judgment part we do have control over. We can accept Christ as our personal savior and receive the rewards stored up for us, or we can ignore the salvation he offers. If we do the latter, there is no escape from the awful result (Heb. 2:3). It is a "dreadful thing to fall into the hands of the living God" (Heb. 10:26-31).

I for one do not like to think about bad things. The Bible calls us to renew our mind (Rom 12:2) and think about good things (Phil. 4:8). We are called upon to take our thoughts captive and make them obedient to Christ (2 Cor. 10:5). If we can do that, we can rely on Gal.5:6 giving us all we need in this life, "Faith expressing itself through love". It will also prepare us for the next. Love remains the Real Deal. If we capture that in our thoughts and actions we will be in a right relationship with our creator.

Frequently scripture calls upon us to be reminded of certain things. Let me end this book by reminding you of the three things that remain, "faith, hope, and love. But the greatest of these is love" (1 Cor. 13:13)